D0626450

To Fergal Keane
best wishes
Michael

PEACEKEEPER

8/7/2017

Michael J. Whelan

Doire Press

First published in 2016

Doire Press
Aille, Inverin
Co. Galway
www.doirepress.com

Layout & cover design: Lisa Frank
Cover images: Michael J. Whelan
Author photo: Emily Whelan

Printed by Clódóirí CL
Casla, Co. na Gaillimhe

ISBN 978-1-907682-46-9

CONTENTS

PART I

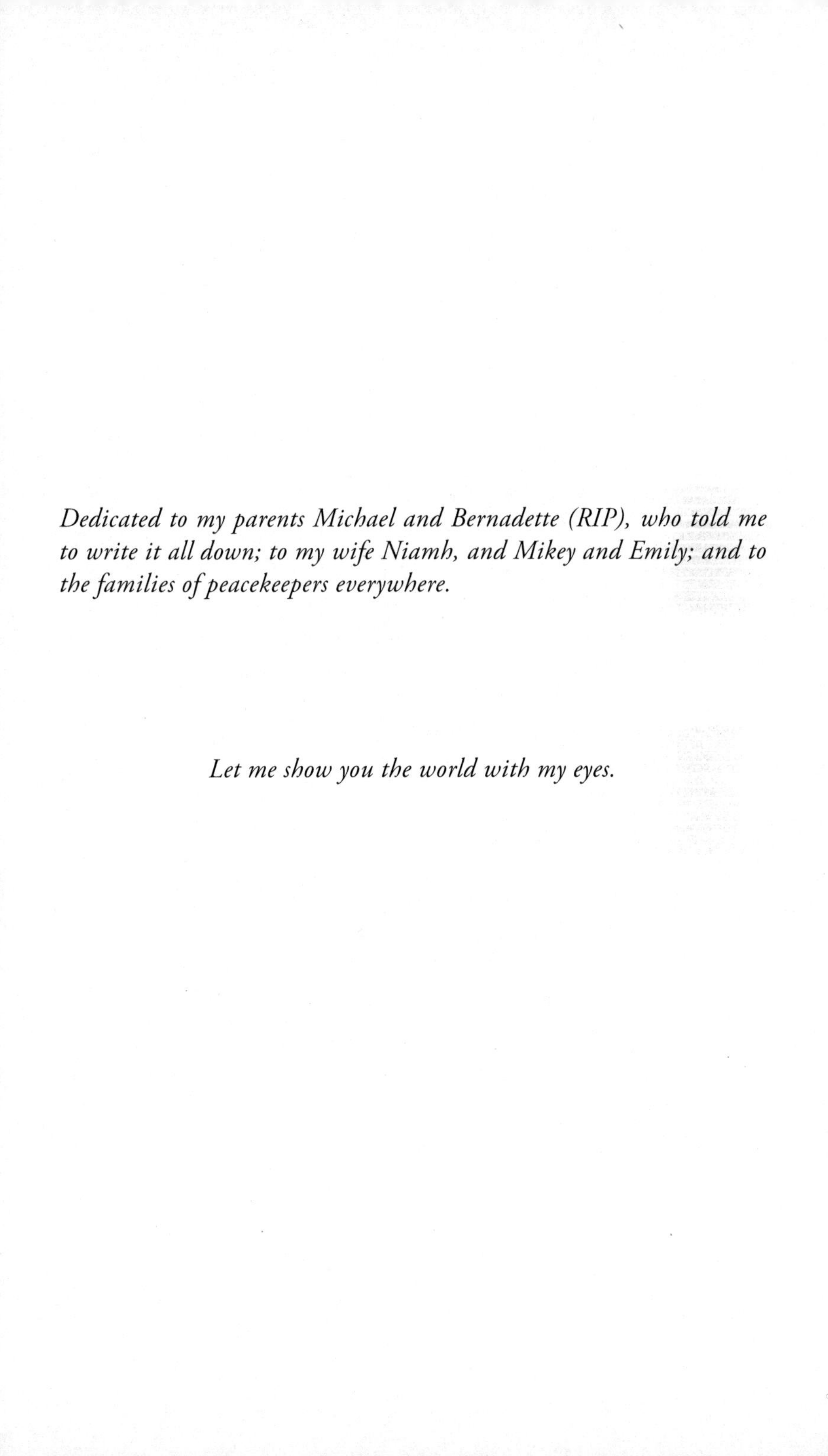

Dedicated to my parents Michael and Bernadette (RIP), who told me to write it all down; to my wife Niamh, and Mikey and Emily; and to the families of peacekeepers everywhere.

Let me show you the world with my eyes.

PART I

'Poets of the west think of Lebanon as a legendary place,
forgotten since the passing of David and Solomon and the
prophets; as the Garden of Eden became lost after the fall of
Adam and Eve. To those western poets, the word "Lebanon" is a poetical
expression associated with a mountain whose sides are drenched
with the incense of the Holy Cedars. It reminds them of the temples of
copper and marble standing stern and impregnable and of
a herd of deer feeding in the valleys. That night I saw Lebanon dream-like
with the eyes of a poet…'

—Kahlil Gibran, *The Broken Wings*, 1912
Al-'Ajniha Al-Mutakassirah

Blue Helmets

The journey from Beirut
to the hills of South Lebanon
was long and hot. The convoy
stopped at Tyre and we debussed
for a piss against the rusted tracks
of an old knocked-out tank.
We were issued our blue helmets
and flak-jackets there, mine were
in really bad shape, like they had been
through the wars.

Critical Outcome

In the quiet before violence
the only bullet a peacekeeper wants
passing through the white chrome of his head
is the imaginary calibre type.
Its direction of approach — unimportant,
the pictures created in his mind
require little skill in determining
the critical outcome of a projectile
as it exits the globe of his skull
over and over again.

This practice is the training his
brain needs to realise that staying
low is the best option
when metal starts flying.

Moral of the Story

for Tony Roe

A convoy of three Mercedes cars and a pick-up
truck fleeing the retaliations of the Israeli
backed militia, which they have just ambushed,
bombs down the hill towards a UN
roadblock in the narrow chicane
of a sun trapped checkpoint
manned by Irish peacekeepers.
Full to the teeth with Hezbollah
Resistance, fighters armed with rocket
propelled grenades and automatic rifles,
and not having time to stop in the stifling
heat of day, the convoy opens up
spraying the checkpoint with bullets
and shrapnel. And the moral of the story?
Peacekeepers in Lebanon may not always
hold the centre ground but they are always
caught in the middle.

First Blood

The higher into the hills you go, the narrower
the roads become and tighter the villages.
The journey slows to a sequence of photographic
scenes in mystical life where you remind yourself
that you are the soldier, peacekeeper,
the alien in this country.
Your convoy crawls through a sea of busy faces,
some study you as they smoke, while others go about
their business and for a moment you're vulnerable
in the circus of a thousand yellow chicks.
The smell of spices hides the faint hint of rotting flesh.
Your body is alive capturing everything in its senses,
the flowing colours you're experiencing dance upon
your eyes and skin as the crowd surrounds you —
your existence is lost in this market-place dream.
The sea parts: hind legs strung up by an old stained cord,
first blood is drawn. A convulsing goat's warm froth pours
down from the gaping throat, pools out onto the gutter-ground.
The wound reminds you that you are not the invader.

Crates stacked high full of yellow chicks are common in the marketplaces/ Souks of South Lebanon.

Irish Batt

Loosened and raised
and settled again,
and again
by constant vibrations,
sandbags split
at imperfect seams
spilling a little,
the sands of time,
sliding onto tired helmets
and wide-eyed
peacekeepers
huddled beneath
ancient bunkers,
built and rebuilt
year on year.

The stars wince
at each titan crash
of metal
against the scarred earth,
fearing for the soldiers
and those they protect.

Troops on the road
man their guns,
tank-stops block junctions
as they watch the circus
of tracer and flash
in phosphorous spectacle
braced against the din.

Prayers to Christ and Allah
drift into the black,
skipping off the conflicted hills

of Irish Batt
and up to the heavens;
the only response
a reign of shells.

The storm is ending,
dancing pebbles are stilled
by the morning sun.
Villages count the innocent,
repair homes,
build their lives again
until the next attack
or battle,
or retaliation.

The Snake Road

Irish area of operations — South Lebanon 1990s

It wound out like the long
wriggling body of a reptile, treacherous.
Most mornings it had to be swept for roadside bombs
by the Early Bird, the snake could bite.
At dawn they would set out,
walking the length of the living thing
with electronic mine detecting gear, slowly,
the lead sweeper swinging the Valon
from left to right continuously,
like a doctor with a stethoscope
listening carefully on ear pieces for a change in tone.
Medics, bomb disposal and armed security elements
following at a safe distance
in case of booby-traps,
it happened many times,
all under the scornful guns of warring factions.
The only protection a blue flag
that didn't always work.

Tour of Duty

There is this memory of violence,
this sand on Tel Aviv Beach,
like warm powder between my toes,
what I imagine the moon is like
when warmed by the sun, and I stand there,
white waves rolling in like silent dreams
I haven't had yet, the sea distorting the curve.

I wake suddenly to a bluc sky,
welcome myself again to the great
encapsulating dome of reality,
the peace torn by a low flying jet
dropping strings of chaff, bursting
through the valley to hide safely behind the hills,
mission complete, ordnance delivered over Beirut.

I welcome myself back again,
collect my bearings,
remember where it is I am.

The pilot will be home soon.
I count the days.

Rank

Sometimes armoured cars
pulled bodies
from wadiis,
a farmer tending his crops,
a herdsman his flock,
a resistance fighter
blown apart and perforated,
black and bloated in the heat,
rank and crawling with life
and difficult to lasso.

Wadii: dried-up riverbed/valley.

An Irish Peacekeeper on the Coast Road Driving South from Lebanon to Isreal

What are these years if not an instant in eternity?
This earthly life and all therein is but a dream
by the side of the awakening we call by death and terror.
A dream, yet all we see and do therein
endures with God's enduring.

— Kahlil Gibran

Eyes closed and I'm there
cruising along the coast road
in the back of a white soft-topped UN jeep,
rifle at my knee, sun warming my face,
burning my outstretched arm
in the open window.

Date-palms shoot past, their curved fronds
breaking the blue sky, the historic sea
on my right shoulder.
Salt air fills my lungs in place of dirt and dust,
the border's getting closer,
this place is still beautiful.

I know there are palm trees like these
all over The South,
a few cedar groves too in the *Chouf* Mountains,
on Mount Lebanon itself
though not as many as there once were
when their numbers shaded the ancient Bedouin
roaming the *Levant* on well-worn caravan routes
through Sidon and Tyre to the gates of Jerusalem,
resting sometimes in the great Bekaa Valley,
shepherds grazing their flocks.

This is the land of the Canaanites,
the Phoenicians who traded from these beaches and ports
and I know it can never be as it was.
Alexander's siege of Beirut can still be heard
in the tracks of a tank that replaced the chariot,
the bullet that replaced the arrow,
the rise and fall of empires.

These are the Holy Lands of books, of Scripture and Sura,
the hills where crusaders marched and Islam stood its ground,
where great armies clashed while vultures circled overhead
and craters mark horizons to Judea.

I come in peace not victorious or triumphant,
no palms will be thrown under my feet
when I enter the City of David.
I open my eyes
and it's twenty years later.

Mosaic

On a journey into clay a small neat hole reveals
where the bullet connects with flesh,
his eyes disbelieving. In the distance a heavy calibre
gun drills the air like a jack-hammer, pumping scorched
lead into a burning landscape.

Bullets coning towards enemy targets pick out the
unlucky peacekeeper patrolling the buffer zone between
life and death. In that moment far across the valley both
shooter and victim are drawn together forever by the spitting
flash of rifled barrel and the muzzled bark that sends the
projectile to pierce his chest.

The exit is painted on the ground like a mosaic of blood
and bone and gristle as metal smashes through his body,
wrenching the sternum that protects his heart and vertebrae
that held the soldier moments before while he thought of home.
He lies there peering at a foreign sky, blood spilling from
his mouth, a gaping hole in his back.

Portal

It is the quiet time.
We have disturbed a hornet's nest.
Sandbags give shape to the sand.
We fill them in pairs,
one holding the mouth open
the other bending into a bridge over the earth,
the spade lifting grains of time as they pour away,
escaping like blood from an open wound.
The rest is just history
shovelled down the neck of a hungry war feeding
on souls, a monster that's never satisfied.

We rest now and then,
catch our breaths, switch tasks,
wipe silver beads from our foreheads with burnt forearms,
stretch our backs, curse the Gods and warmed bottled water.

We fill sandbags with the erosion of time.
Pile them, shape them and square them off
around the bunker.
Life is shorter for the hornet.

I think of its shiny green body,
remembering how it dug into the sand, pushing with its legs,
as we are digging now with shoulders arching in the sun.
The hornet is dead.

The bunker has a doorway in the shade,
a portal to the underworld
when the sky is filled with lead
and we become creatures of the dark.

Grapes of Wrath

It happens on a Thursday, just after 2pm,
when ancient cultures and beliefs conspire
and vultures spiral above a peacekeepers' camp,
where cedars age slowly and the *Litani* River
caresses the ground where Jesus turned water
into wine, where artillery salvos rip the air
on their long flight and bite deep, deep into
that place of safety vaporizing its concrete
walls and burning and blistering and tearing
apart the mass of terrified flesh and innocent blood
seeking refuge from the hate of man.

A soldier climbs from the rubbled limbs
and discarded faces, his eyes caked black with tears,
his hands at arm's length clutching the newborn baby
that looks like a headless doll.

(Qana Massacre April 18th, 1996)
During 'Operation Grapes of Wrath' Israeli Defence Force artillery shells struck a Fijian UN compound in South Lebanon protecting 800 civilians fleeing the fighting, approximately 120 died.

Hill 880

Irish UN position — South Lebanon

Tonight, senses steeled against
the black sky, we listen for the warring
shadows. The storm is almost upon us.
Bursts of coloured tracer attack the hill,
bouncing over lost horizons.
Phosphorous lights explode,
illuminating battered landscapes of death.
Below the thunder they cower
in the dancing veil again and again.

They who do battle here fear this night also.
But we who keep the middle ground will feel
the vibrations of their vengeance.
Our presence does not halt their conflict.
Braced against the fury, we don our blue
helmets, cursing, send prayers to mothers
a thousand miles away.
The ground trembles beneath our rising flares,
burning red against the moonless heavens,
"WE ARE HERE, WE ARE HERE.
FIRING CLOSE, FIRING CLOSE."

Deliverance

In the orphanage a child
cowers from cursing men outside.
She wants to climb back into
her dead mother's womb
and hide inside its warm, soft,
un-edged safety,
where no explanation is needed
or reason to hide under splintered
staircases or run the gauntlet to basement
bomb shelters, existing minute to minute
with strangers until the dawn arrives with her
deliverance and she refuses to be born.

Khamsin Winds

She lies in cold mourning, under heated breaths.
Row on row the streetlight halos gather thoughts
and eyes to see the hands of those who lived here once.

Death is preying in her streets again
crying towards the night.
This city, this church, this perfect cathedral
is but a crypt under the corbelled roofs of passage tombs
and pyramids to the past.

The charnel pillars that hours before cooked breakfast,
opened shops, brought children to school
are waiting for the Khamsin winds to come,
to bury their ashes in desert sands,
carry the embers to heaven.

With those who built these walls
they are ascending always, an illusion to the future,
only the present will speak their names,
only that which they create might linger to see the dusk,
the shop front windows reflect the dying sun
like daylight mirrors reminding their ghosts of yesterdays
and the promise of tomorrows.

The Soldier's Face

after Qana,
identification

In the sitting room of corpses
there is no ceiling.
A soldier pulls two from the rubble,
lays them side by side
on the un-buried coffee table,
kneels before them,
washes their tiny limbs
with hard water,
wipes dust from their eyes,
metal from their mouths.

He will not look up,
still trying to protect them.

Salim (his name means safe)
searches for his daughters,
his ears are still ringing.
The words he does not want to hear
are written on the soldier's face.

Revelation

Lebanon

This is the land of giants, where Gilgamesh
raped the mountains of cedars,
the place where the peacekeeper reads the landscape
like he reads the skin of the people, their faces,
their telling eyes.

The trees are almost gone, the remnants bleached
by the sun and carrying deformities of a thousand years
like the skin of the old ones
who don't remember how it is to be happy,
to be free, to be young.

This is the place of death and the living,
the conflict of ideologies,
the world and all its misery.
It is the place of broken hearts.

I want to push my bloody hands into sand,
see my fingers cleansed by an ocean of grains.
I want to dig up the Templar tombs,
find the place of Saladin and show them
all that they have sown.

And if I am to die here then let this landscape take me
for now at last I know
the reason why I have come.

Distant Whisper

Do you remember
how drops of water
trickle down stone walls
in the *wadiis* of South Lebanon,
as they have for a thousand years,
over contours, between grooves,
slowing on rough rendering?
How it reminded you of the West of Ireland,
white lines on her hills?

Do you remember
liquid moving like a teardrop,
trickling in a whisper of life,
the hum of a bee, or an insect
living in its own significance,
going about its business
as time stands still
long enough for you to study
the erosion of war,
knowing that a belt of Point Five ammunition
fired at you could turn this feature to rubble
in an instant?

Do you remember thinking
if you die here today — behind this old wall,
trickles will go on forming slow grooves
and you will be that distant whisper?

Inshalla

Seest thou not how Allah Coineth a Similitude:
A goodly saying, as a goodly tree, its roots set firm,
branches reaching into heaven.

— Qur'an, 14:24

The war is over in the South, again.
Nightingales are singing,
children play under juniper trees
growing on the high ground.

In the villages pictures of the fallen
are posted to windows and walls,
minarets and mosques.

They are the faces of the missing and the dead,
the eyes of the innocent,
protected by weapons and prayers.

They are the eyes of martyred resistance
looking back from the emptiness,
forcing the onlooker to wonder on their fate.

But they are too many,
the old obscured by the new,
the new fading quickly in the sunlight.

I will not remember the faces,
only the word *Inshalla*
sticks in my brain and to my lips,
'Inshalla' — Allah be willing,
where it is written
beneath the painting of a cedar tree.

The Cinder Bus

Hebron, Palestinian West Bank —1994

Above me a jet
leaves a long scratch
on a perfect sky.

The crowds pour out,
the shutters come down,
the town changes shape.

Then comes the shouts,
the stones,
the bottles and bricks

smashing into shuttered shop fronts
and the patrolling Israeli soldiers
channelling through the streets

in a slow verse of history,
into the familiar well-rehearsed ambush,
this arsenal of new rubble,

this old battleground,
this biblical reverie
of rubber bullets and smoke,

laden down, nervous and young,
hands stuck fast to guns,
helmets hanging on the backs of their heads,

chin-straps between their teeth
like a horse's bit,
frothing at the mouth,

invisible bridles strung out
pulling armoured chariots
through the hail like tired scriptures.

No glory descends on this broken road
as they pass the cinder bus once more,
the sun casting long shadows.

Showing the Flag

Sometimes it felt peaceful
in the hills above South Lebanon.
Minarets called the faithful to prayers
and in the mornings when clouds
hung like fruit,
you could almost pick them from the sky.

On sunny days on patrol
showing the flag,
local men greeted you with
'Marhaba Irish, keefek sadiki,'
and invited you into the shade
of their houses with hot cups of *chai*,
their wives and daughters offering you figs
and dates,
'*Shoukran, shoukran'* you said
over and over to their smiles,
'Ahlan wa Sahlan'
was always their reply,
the smell of tobacco mixed with olive oil
somehow helped you relax.

Sometimes in the evenings
unmarried girls trooped up and down
the streets in front of young men and boys
as peacekeepers observed.

Funeral

South Lebanon

It's thirty-five degrees — boots off,
too hot to work outside, too tired to move.
I'm watching the recording of a World Cup
soccer clash.

Giant black flies begin to attack
crawling on my feet,
the more of them I kill
the less peace they give.
I have an arsenal of names for them,
they treat me like the dead.

On the road above my billet
the Resistance is marching.
I see them through the window,
all dressed in funeral black,
hear them yelling and chanting,
slapping their chests.

They swarm around pick-up trucks
and Mercedes cars,
sporting RPGs and automatic weapons,
bursting the heavens with gunfire,
another martyr is on his way.

Piles of bodies hold the floor at my feet,
the newspaper is blood-smeared
but still they come,
the weapon no good against the tide.

The funeral is louder, more intense,
all commentary lost in emotions,
I reach for my helmet and gun,
in a moment the shells will start falling.

The Tide

Silver bodies float on the surface
driftwood — reflecting the sun.
Soldiers fish with hand grenades
as shadow birds cluster
flying on white sands under water.

I stand on the feet of my shadow
arms outstretched — resting on a still sea,
bearing no weapons,
the tide is undecided.

Identity discs hang from my neck
tangled up with miraculous medal,
scapula and crucifix.
I was the peacekeeper.

The tide is turning.

Centuries Keep Watch

Inside our wire
a great anthill keeps the curved ground rising,
an army breaking the horizon
behind the sandbagged wall.
We are nothing to it
except when we too seek shelter
beneath the tremoring ground
and the big guns point our way.

Outside the bunker centuries keep watch,
while columns of soldier-ants
reach far into the future and the past,
their long black lines marching up
and down the mountain over this defence post,
conquering palisades, barbed wire and borders,
pouring through cracks in reinforced blast walls,
in and out like a two-way shipping route
with the carved-up parts of their enemies
and the spoil of a million wars.

If I was to smash this colony with my rifle
where then would the fair winds take its remains,
would it leave dust on the roof of my mouth,
its scouts swarming through my nights
in a rage of retribution?

Where I Am

I should be here
but I'm not.
I'm clinging to her face
a thousand miles away in the past,
her hands in mine,
head resting on her soft breasts,
counting her heartbeats,
lying on crumpled sheets
under a warm sun
filling my room,
that's where I am.

Far from barbed wire and gabions,
tank-stops and piercing cold nights
and the shelling
'cause I've had enough,
that's where I am.

Paradox of the Peacekeeper in the Holy Land

I am forever walking upon the shore
betwixt the sand and the foam.
The high tide will erase my footprints,
and the wind will blow away the foam,
but the sea and the shore will remain forever.

— Kahlil Gibran

In Lebanon I sought redemption
like the pilgrim at the crossroads of Heliopolis,
on the Bekaa's great range where Bedouin caravans met
and Romans laid their bodies down in supplication to their gods,
to Aphrodite and Jupiter, and long before this peacekeeper came
on what seemed a fool's errant, whose only armour
was the feeble weave of a blue flag,

before these wars for modernity and religion
where the new city's shadows fall like dead soldiers
on the broken steps of Astarte's Temple,
where the priests of Baalbek burned incense,
laid themselves prostrate with tribute and homage
beseeching fertility over the land and on warriors on the eve of battle

and the same priests parcelled out her favours to believers
who built new columns to the Sun God on her ruins,
before all this there was blood on the stones and in the dust
of Tyre, of Sidon and in Byblos,
and the gods looked down from the heavens and laughed
for they knew that man knew not of their fallibilities,
their eyes kept the storms that belief constructed —

the defence of Masada by Jewish zealots
against ramparts, siege-towers and battering rams of enemies — never giving in,
the caliphs who ordered the conquests of Bilad al-Sham,
Helen who setting forth from Constantinople to Jerusalem
in search of the Cross set beacons ready to burn along the way
and Constantine, her son, converted his empire in promise to his mother

who lit the path for Crusaders and the burial places of a thousand years
under these skies of mumatus clouds that hang like fronds of fruit
above the hills at dusk, who rest like relics with Saracens
and Mamluks, the swords of east and west,
the holy books of Abraham, Mohamed and Byzantium,
where Gilgamesh cleaved the cedars for his ships

and where now the free man might dig with trowels once more,
adjure in the Temple of Baachus, revere the flake-bones of gladiators
under the triumphal arch of Al-Minah — the hippodrome at Tyre,
where fishermen still cast their nets on the same Phoenician shore
in Galilee beneath the stirring sands of Jordan
and camels sometimes carry scholars through the Quadisha Valley
like in the old days passing slopes of red anemone, wild tulip, oleander and poppy

and young girls might seek the damask rose in the gorges of forgotten ambushes,
where sultans and kings slaked their pious thirsts — slew their enemies
and exiled the youth of many futures — those pawns who lay penitent at the altars,
who lay down in the Temple of Aphrodite like the peacekeepers lie down now,
yes we who lie down with our wives and lovers like knights with sacred talismans
and far away they lie down with us under the same different moons,

they wait and pray looking up upon the many faces of the Gods
who see us only as a fleeting moment on the pages of passing civilizations,
the rising and setting of the sun and we know the signal fires are burning,
the funeral pyres rise up in pillars of ash in the marches between the watchtowers
along the border wire and we know that so much metal has been fired in this cauldron
from arrowheads and spears to icons and the corrupted jagged shards of bombs,
shrapnelled landmines and bullets. On a rainy day we can almost smell it
weeping through the red mud tracks of an army and we must watch our step.

Splintered

i.m. of all peacekeepers killed in Lebanon

Amplify the instant of this temporal link,
living your days,
walking above the living ground
breathing air that I breathed.
Give light to me
in your sacred hearth,
hang me in its peaceful corners
that I may fan the sails
of your curtained heart.
For I am stilled,
captured in bursting flames
and scorched metal
piercing curved retinas
that once photographed you,
reflect your silhouette still
and fragment this body,
these dreams,
into a million splintered memories.

Phospherous Dreams

The long shadows invade our space as she sleeps,
inhaling cool breeze under sail-shaped curtains,
I watch her till I drift.

Early morning attack goes in,
suicidal resistance sucks the air,
I hold my breath and watch the din.

The black is broken to my sight,
flashes of floating bouncing light,
necklaces of orange and green trace the night
streaming toward each other from the dark.

Radio traffic panics the glare,
one of our posts is under fire,
great clouds of blue smoke, coiling wire,
blast walls and bunkers,
sandbags vibrate across the floor.

Red flares cut the sky.
My lover lies naked, I hear her voice,
her body a sea in silent moonlight,
she moves me like perfect sand dunes in the dark.

The walls are punctured, villages tremor to mortars coughs.
The hills are waking — the quiet explodes in deafening sound.
I wade through hot liquid,
the ground moves to a constant crash,
she reaches out, rests my dreams on her skin,
pulls barbed wire from my mouth.

Wild Juice

I search but you're not there,
only this veil of darkness that hides
all the world and you from me.

Far away you're waiting and I am
there, for a moment,
free of gunfire and threat of violence.
I hear your singing and I am drawn
to your touch, watching you eat round
strawberries, resting in long grass
on a summer day, your lips are red
with wild juice and I long to kiss them.
But I close my eyes as the scent of dates
fills my brain, you are hidden again
and I cannot breathe under this black veil.

White stars are like pinholes without air
as night rises over my observation post
and I scan the rooftops through my rifle scope.

Irish Martyrs in Lebanon

after conversations with Lebanese exiles

Some words we don't read them,
we taste them
deep into our souls,
some bring back our missing memories,
our loved ones to our hearts.

Many times I saw their wives and mothers
lay flowers in my country
near the places of their martyrdoms.

My heart is like a room
big enough to receive many visitors.
My heart is a wing
to fly your martyrs on,
to reach heaven

to make them meet at the river,
to hug and kiss their children,
to sacrifice and water their thirsts
for a land with pure blood
spilled far from home

flowing from peacekeepers
into the valleys of my country
where the cedar grows forever
and remembers everything.

PART II

'My fellow Americans, today our Armed Forces joined our NATO allies in airstrikes against Serbian forces responsible for the brutality in Kosovo. We have acted with resolve for several reasons. We act to protect thousands of innocent people in Kosovo from a mounting military offensive. We act to prevent a wider war, to diffuse a powder keg at the heart of Europe that has exploded twice before in this century with catastrophic results. And we act to stand united with our allies for peace. By acting now, we are upholding our values, protecting our interests, and advancing the cause of peace.'

— Bill Clinton, Statement on Kosovo (March 24, 1999)

Field of Blackbirds

The carrion of dead innocents
picked over by a murder of crows
that holds ill court
over who lives
and who dies
fertilizes the *Field of Blackbirds.*

Field of Blackbirds: one of the ancient names for Kosovo.

Kosovo

Green shoots
why do you grow
in the rubble of this house,
while hearts are breaking?
Does God not see
our tears falling on the ground
near the stony road
that ceases at one side of the river
and commences on the other,
where great armies once crossed
to be forgotten,
in this land that forged a village
and civilised it
then forged the swords
that killed it,
where the blackbird died slowly
in the eagle's grip,
screaming as the beak
pierced the flesh of its breast?

Liberators

Sometimes (in Kosovo), you can drive into villages
feeling like a liberator.
Though at first the children are standoffish,
weary of uniforms, they learn why
the Irish K.FOR have come and slowly
trickle down from high ground
and surround you.
It gets difficult to work then, unloading sand
and cement, building blocks and slates
from giant trucks,
so the drivers organise races, throwing chocolates
and sweets from our pack-rations as prizes.

On other days you can enter ancient villages
stopping close to mass graves, their hurting ground.
It takes a lot of persuasion for children
to come down, there aren't many parents around
to tell them they're safe.
It is then you feel enfeebled.

K.FOR: Kosovo Peacekeeping Force.

This is the Day

Balkans

Narrow lines of yellow tape
stretch up into forest hills
marking places where it's safe to trek
between unexploded bombs
and dead refugees waiting to be rescued.

This is the day
a peacekeeper is blown to bits
clearing a path to a suspected mass grave
near an empty village,
where booby-trapped doors wait to be opened,
made safe before the houses might live again.

His friends finish the search
before gathering all the parts of him,
zipping them into a dozen body bags,
each soldier sweating in his own skin
relieved it wasn't him,
as the dead look on.

The Family

Kosovo

There were nine of them.
Eight children under the age of ten,
existing in the rough shell
of a house with a hole in its roof
and a young mother, whose
sanity had run out.

I stood there in the bowel of
her existence,
slack-jawed in the middle
of that frozen room,
rifle under my arm.
It was Christmas time at home.

How do I sort this out?
No one can threaten hunger with bullets.

Tiny hands were in my pockets.
I gave her my watch.

Echoes

There is nothing left in this village
but the burnt out shells of homes,
roofless rooms and echoes
drifting across scorched black grass,
following boot prints through alleyways
and well-trodden streets,
over rank smelling chicken coops,
dead pigs and silent tractors
stuck in time and sodden earth,
past the ancient cemetery and schoolhouse
to a raised ditch on the side of an infamous hill,
where the only living things without guilt
are the swarming swollen flies
feasting on the end story of a thousand years.

The echoes are not of children's laughter!

Search and Destroy

Djakovica Massacre
Kosovo — March 1999

'They came in the night,'
Besa said, holding the buggy tight.
'We were scared, hiding between
buildings and under floors.
We ran from house to house
through holes in walls,
it was dangerous to go through doors!

They burned our homes,
with our people inside,
and there by the stream,
see there is Mendi and Teki,
my cousins with the others
forming a hill of corpses
and in the old marketplace
you will see the broken cobbles
filled with blood.

I am alive — see, this is my child.
I covered her mouth with my hand
like this, till the shooting ended.
I am alive but I am not happy.'

Bad Days

The mist peels back for the rainfall,
I feel the craziness once more.

In the wild eyes of an old man's face
I see his mirrored thoughts
fouled by the bad days just gone,
still trapped here in this place.

The sky is falling,
lingering mist slowly reveals pain
as it clings to leafless treetops.
Each breath I take is different
every one he takes the same.

The closer I come to the stone,
to the fabric — to the tales
gripping this village
the lonelier I become,
my ears want to hear,
my eyes to see
but my heart says 'no'.

There is groaning
in the empty doorway,
my stomach tightens,
he is calling to his wife.
I button up my combat jacket,
shove my hands deep into pockets,
make fists that no-one sees.

She will not come,
his heart is breaking again.
I step back,
back out into the sucking mud.

The Witness You Once Were

The place is in the periphery of memories,
the objects that bring you back,
in the outer elements,
the noise beyond buildings,
the bodies in landscapes,
underground whispers licking at you
from waving crops
speaking your name on the breeze,
seeking you out,
in those voices are the moments,
the witness you once were.

On the far side of the road,
just out of sight
is the heart skipping a beat
on captured breaths,
the days you never tried to forget
but left behind anyway.

You feel them sometimes
a darkness drawing you in and then
you're walking the cemetery fields again,
afraid that you're insulting the dead
whose only wish is to be found,
who pull the blanket ground over their heads
because outside these visions that hold you is the truth,
they know many years have passed
since they last saw the light and you don't want to return.

Tread Softly

It's raining, always is,
that sticky hazy rain that gets down your neck,
behind your ears and saturates your face, your hair
as soon as you step from the vehicle
even though the uniform is multilayered,
your boots get soggy straight away
and the pistol grip on the rifle resting in your arms
slips in your fist.

You're not really afraid — for yourself,
though your heart is racing as you approach
the recently finished mass grave — their hurting ground
covered in fresh clay, flags and wreaths.
You've just driven over the ancient village cemetery as you entered
like it was a cross country speed test on rough terrain,
the old grave markers are long gone.

No, you're not afraid for yourself,
the fear comes when no adult arrives to greet you
or check out your party as a possible threat
save for the elderly ones corralling young children
behind hedges and outhouses on the high ground,
who watch you as you watch them,
barefoot and half dressed in the rain,
watch you taking photographs of yourselves
at the place of their parents.

You — the uniforms that stormed into their hurting ground
feeling like liberators but to them resembling conquerors,
you who come to help but instead bring memories of terror
and usher a fear they keep from the last time
soldiers conquered this place,
you who tread softly then when you realize what you have done,
when you see the muddied feet of innocence and the future in their eyes.

The Rain Has Come

The war is long over but it is not ended.
The searchers have come again
to dig but they must wait,
for today will be made of sorrow and pain.

The rain is falling, contaminated by gunpowder and
the residue of long decayed firebombed trees
rolling down into ditches and the gullies of dried-up riverbeds,
where the wind might sometimes lift the ghosts of the dead
into whispering dust devils to live and die once more
within the span of moments.

The rain has come
to wash away the footprints of killers
and the hopes of the hurting,
who still long for the missing,
their hearts hinged on a rusting bullet casing
exposed like a white bone on the deepening red mud.

Through the Steyr AUG (Army Universal Gun) 1.5X Optical Sights

The Steyr assault rifles 1.5x telescopic sights contain a simple black ring reticule with basic range finder designed that at 300m a 5.9ft tall man size target will completely fill it, giving the shooter an accurate method of estimating range.

At 300 meters
each man fills the reticule
in the optical sights of the assault rifle,
just observing — not shooting,
though later in my mind's eye
it looks as if I'm taking aim
as they sharpen knives from a rolled up satchel
and pull a goat by the neck to the gutter.

Bones trapped in the hard dirt
along these village roads
could fill a great ossuary
of unremembered lives
that come and go here
but there is no such repository
to the sacrificed
missing every year from the fields at harvest.

The ground knows well of their passing
and will never tell their whereabouts.

The Bridge

It's in the dying that their lives have meaning.
You never knew this could happen
but as you cross the bridge into their world
the story of that landscape precedes them,
the ground pushes on your very being,
you feel the tragedies of that place.

The river is the flicker sound,
the noise of passed tribulations
rushing under arches
and you realize then
that your rescue is too late,
your charge no good
except to save in your own mind
the murder of innocence.

They have no faces
though you imagine the play
of their last moments over and over
as the trees gather about you, rustling,
whispering as the war reveals itself.

There are no bodies, no blood, no greetings,
only the memories of what happened
in that far away empty space
and those memories aren't even yours.

Broken Spade

You lay in your frozen field, slack-jawed at how you
came to be there, your mouth caked in last year's mud,
limbs twisted about your body as if in the midst of some
remembered dance or tempered at your rotting crops,
bent over in disgust, yielding in the half light and startled
at the cold they have never felt.

This harvest, un-reaped and yet reaped upon you
hides the stale shoe and crushed spectacles,
the broken spade that hastily covered you in the soft
clay you loved, now steeled hard against the sharp sky.

I imagine the fears of your kin as they searched the high
golden horizon that summer day.
They might have felt the distant calamity that took you
following the bullet casings along the beaten track.
And I wonder if they found you?
Then I see the scars of cluster bombs and scorched
stalks of your petrified labours and there, there in the shrapnel
of this bitter harvest I behold your seed,
torn apart but reaching out to the one who bore them.

Roadside Bomb

Torn into shreds, metal fused to flesh and flesh
to metal borne, veins and skin dripping,
unwrapping from bones,
legs hanging from roof windows,
arms stretched out as if shaking hands with their
murderer or waving, others swimming in boiling
blood pooling between half-bodied seats
and broken conversations,
their own bewildered faces looking on.

We had felt the tremor but took no notice,
you get used to that after a while, though we heard
the details later, how they'd timed it perfectly under
a bus full of mourners, ripping it apart in the centre
of a convoy of peacekeepers as it crossed over
the border to a cemetery where their loved ones lived
safely, under the ground in one piece,
waiting on the old.

February 17th 2001: Serbian Orthodox Church's annual Day of the Dead.
A Serbian bus is blown up while being escorted by NATO armoured vehicles into Kosovo.

Chocolate

Her face worn and haggard,
she lay across the muddy floor
next to a filthy child,
protecting a barren door,
her weak hands smashing nuts
with a broken hammer.

Dark clouds hung inside
the shattered house,
her silent eyes screaming at us
while our trucks dropped supplies
to her guilty neighbours.

With cold despair clinging to our uniforms
we spilled mountains of chocolate
at her feet.

In Kosovo peacekeepers wouldn't always know, when first entering towns and villages, that the occupants there were often responsible for atrocities and ill-treatment of each other. These atrocities usually fell across ethnic divides.

Cold Rubble

Jehona, the old woman
promised safety,

weeps on a puddled
floor (her name means Echo)

half-buried under cold rubble
that once framed a house

the anti-tank mine
booby-trapping a door destroyed

she kisses the face of her grandson
Kushtrine (his name means Battle-Cry),

holding his head
tight to her breast,

his shrapnel body lashed to the ruins
and mixed with false promises.

Silent Convoys

Playing fields and roadsides still
hide their prize
flat-packed strata
in the hard coveting earth
layer upon layer
limbs and possessions mingling
in an overcrowded place.

Sometimes we watched
from silent convoys
listening for the word to come
the searchers digging for what once
were boys and men
longing to feel the day's breath
on their bony faces
to hold up their skeleton arms
and call out to those who love them still:
Here I am, here I am,
            come, take me home.

The Place She Will Not Walk

Pusto Selo Massacre
Kosovo, 26 June 1999

Believe the emptiness when you see it
the pain that saturates soil with souls
of the half living.

Believe it when a husband praying for his sons
collects acorns for his wife at the place she will not walk
under an old tree devoid of leaves still bending into
the shape of yesterday's storms
sheltering proud saplings and scraping the sky
like a harrowed claw, its own seed long fallen.

Believe that she has no more to give the world
when she plants them in the ground
next to her heart.

Prishtina

It was only a moment
but he looked into me.
Could see me as clearly
as I see him after all this time,
his eyes piercing my soul,
digging deep.

I'm at a main junction in Prishtina,
my jeep is turning left into
the raging river highway
near the barracks flattened by
NATO bombers a few months before.

I'm counting satellite dishes that
seemed to overpopulate the high-rise
landscape overnight,
a sign of normality at last perhaps?

The rusty orange car catches my attention.
Starting and stopping in a crazy fashion,
like a piece of farmyard machinery that
hasn't seen a road in years, fuelled with
kangaroo juice, its driver on the loose.

I caught his eyes then, as he lay across
the back seat. The agony in his face as they
reached out to me and I saw what remained
of his leg. The ball of his knee hanging,
attached by loose skin and gristle
and wrapped in a bloody white shirt.

Our drivers took control then and sped
in opposite directions. I couldn't help him
but I know he sees me,
like I can see dead people.

The Chicken Farm

After reveille in Camp Clark
the ground raised itself up,
moved around the *Chicken Farm* camp
of guano that nearly always stank
and bred flies brave enough to attack
our eyes and hovered as if we were
the walking dead.

They assaulted in force from a cesspit trench
dug in the cold dirt outside the wire
and we were unable to eat,
arms crossed over defending our plates
against their swarming dives
while others tried to snatch morsels
from our mouths.

That day the ground lifted towards us
with a million mice, like locusts,
eating all the earth.

Camp Clarke: Irish Transport Coy Head Quarters Kosovo 2000/01 was built on the site of an operating chicken farm.

The Invisible

Like territory and the dead,
the missing too have value in the spoils of war.
Taken from homes, from streets and fields
they vanish, invisible but not forgotten.
They become leveraged, a reason to prolong
conflict, a reason for reprisal and hate.
And so the ground takes new purchase
on belligerent hearts, the search for truth
as always has a blood price.

Revenge

Coming to relieve
the victims of ethnic cleansing,
they heard the echoes of revenge
that smashed the altars of Gracanica
and cemeteries of Pec,
burned the houses of Obilic
and Urosevec,
the gunfire that trod upon
the old man
face down in the river
of tears.

Arms

During the war in Kosovo
a lot of ordnance was dropped,
the ground sown with a
deadly liberation.

The children didn't understand,
the merchants never cared.

The children came almost daily,
in all weathers and none,
filthy and cold, traipsing deep
puddle footprints in the melting snow,
smiles empty, arms filled with cluster
bombs and unexploded shells
of one kind or another, from one side
or the other, for the tin merchant
close to our base.

If we gave them money to stop
they just brought more,
if we ignored them, they tapped on the wire
for hours with the contents of their hands.

Outside the base was an UXO pit
our engineers regularly destroyed
when it filled up with
the ticking harvest.

It was hard
some of us had kids at home.

UXO: Unexploded Ordnance.

Rendezvous

The sodden fields are bleak, the road
is broken and I am tired.
Rain shoots off my weary face,
its cold tears count the ribs
that cage my distant heart.
At night I make my rifle safe,
fling this conflict to the floor,
it gathers round the worn-out boots
that tread in miseries of a war.

But I have a rendezvous,
a memory in a future place.
That short black dress, golden hair
tumbling to her shoulders.
Lying foetal, arms wrapping
her soft body, kissing the curve of her
neck, I breathe her in, capturing her.

Base

They stood there — a silent performance,
as if they had feelings,
human feelings,
despondent,
like unfinished pieces
of modern art left to the elements

and it always seemed
that I could smell them
from any corner of the base,
two white forty-foot cold containers
bearing the United Nations mark

that carried the victims of a cleansing
from the badlands to the morgue
and their final resting place,
discarded between movements,
like memorials to the dead, rusting,

the stench ever-present,
the gunk on the doors — a reminder
of what the body returns to.

And when I look into puddled water
I remember trying to clean my boots
and spitting out the taste.

Question

Kosovo 1999

There is a theory, one which I tend to like,
which states 'energy can never die,
always has been, always will be,
only changes form,'
in the same way emotions
built upon events
become something else.

So my question is
are the tears that rolled down
the young boy's face onto bloody ground
when cluster bombs accidently fell on his village
(dropped by those who had come to help)
transformed in some way
and if so
what have they become?

Retribution

Sieges of Balkan Cities

Inside the citadel
cinders flickered in the dusk,
sparks rose up from the ashes
like desperate ghosts escaping the future.

Outside, on the gathering hills,
while the city smoked,
the embers of burning history
glowed in the growing dark.

Out there you huddled with your great guns
around the warmth of thirsty fires,
boots off, souls circling the forgiving heat
as you vanquished past enemies,
relived victories, dismissed defeats
and gloried in the new justice
your liberations would soon bring
to the people within.

The conquered would learn to accept
their new landscapes,
and you their liberators tapped cigarettes
into empty fingerprint shell casings
building up behind your crusade
a brass trail of stained retribution
for all the world to see.

Silent Faces

What right have I to feel despair?
I have come to help,
to witness, to see what they see,
feel what they feel,
in this country of the damned,
this land of agony that chokes itself,
destroys its children and ploughs
the soil of shallow graves,
hiding the pregnant ground that keeps
within its wombs the seed of future
conflicts and future hate,
its secrets and its truths.
I will go home before the end,
forget the grey faces,
the silent faces,
and the tears that fill my heart
may call out to me no more.

Children Standing Fast

If you could see the sunken faces
of children standing fast
at wells and mountain passes,
at unmarked sights,
eyes glazed over,
elbows tight,
reliving the fear
of distant nights,
then you would not laugh
or say in jest
that certain castes
were better dead.

No-Man's Land

The peacekeeper guards his post
observing the past,
the same ground of ancient wars —
this *No-Man's Land.*

He hears the whispers of remorse
from dead leaves,
falling on secret cemeteries.

There is no end to old stories
and he sees in the sand
the page where his part is written.

ACKNOWLEDGEMENTS

Acknowledgements are due to the following publications in which versions of many of these poems were published: *And Agamemnon Dead: An Anthology of Early 21 Century Irish Poetry* (Paris); *A New Ulster*; *Bare Hands Poetry*; *Cyphers*; *InTallaght Magazine*; *New Irish Writing — Irish Independent*; *Paragram* (UK); *Poethead*; *Poetica*; *Poetry Ireland Review*; *Revival*; *Tallaght Echo*; *Tallaght Express*; *Tallaght Soundings — Anthology of New Work by Virginia House Writers (1&2)*; *The Burning Bush*; *The Galway Review*; *The Hundred Years War — Anthology of Modern War Poems* (Bloodaxe UK); *The Penny Dreadful*; *The Poetry Bus*; *Three Monkeys*; *The Moth*; *The Ofi Press* (Mexico); *Outburst* and *Wordlegs.*

I am grateful to the South Dublin County Council Arts Office for the award of an Arts Bursary, to Carolann Copland at Carousel Creates Writers' Centre for the award of a weekend writing retreat, to Tallaght Community Council for the Arts and Culture award in the Tallaght Person of the Year Awards, to Poetry Ireland for selecting me to read at the Poetry Ireland/Eigse Eireann Introductions Series and the workshop with Alan Jude Moore in 2012. I am also grateful to Kieran Swords (RIP), Sile Coleman, Collette Allen and the staff of South Dublin Libraries, the Red Line Book Festival for all of their support, Dr Rosaleen Dwyer — Heritage Officer SDCC, Maria Wallace and the Virginia House Creative Writers, Eileen Casey and Platform One Writers, Peter O'Neill and the Gladstone Readers for all their encouragement over the years. Thanks are also due firstly to my wife Niamh and children Mikey and Emily, and to my family; to Brigadier General Paul Fry — General Officer Commanding Irish Air Corps and members of the Irish Defence Forces who I have come to serve with over the years both abroad and at home; to the members of the Roger Casement Branch of the Organisation of National Ex-Servicemen and Women and the Irish United Nations Veterans' Association who have supported me and have come to many of the exhibitions and readings of the poems in this collection; to the many other writers I have come to know who have befriended, supported and inspired me; and to John Walsh and Lisa Frank at Doire Press for believing in these poems.

MICHAEL J. WHELAN has lived in Tallaght with his family for more than thirty-five years. He joined the Irish Defence Forces in 1990, serving on tours of duty as a United Nations Peacekeeper in South Lebanon and with the Peace-Enforcement mission to Kosovo. Keeper of the Irish Air Corps Military Aviation Museum & Collection, he is the author of *The Battle of Jadotville: Irish Soldiers in Combat in the Congo 1961* (South Dublin Libraries, 2006) and *Allegiances Compromised: Faith, Honour and Allegiance — Ex-British Soldiers in the Irish Army 1913-24* (South Dublin Libraries, 2011). He was appointed by the Irish Defence Forces Chief of Staff to the Editorial Committee for 1916 Anniversary Commemorations in 2006 and the United Nations 50th Anniversary of Peacekeeping publications in June 2008. He holds a Masters Degree in Modern History from NUI Maynooth and has received the General Officer Commanding Irish Air Corps Award, the Paul Tissandier Diploma and the Tallaght Person of the Year Award (Arts & Culture section).

Michael's poetry has been widely published, including in *The Hundred Years' War: Anthology of Modern War Poems* (Bloodaxe) and his work was the subject of a centenary of the Great War exhibition entitled *Landscapes Of War & Peace 1914-2014: War Poetry & Peacekeeping* at the South Dublin Libraries/Red Line Book Festival. He won 2nd Place in the Patrick Kavanagh Poetry Awards, 3rd Place in the Jonathan Swift Creative Writing Awards and a commendation in the Carousel Creates Creative Writing Awards, as well as having received an Arts Bursary from South Dublin Arts Office. In 2012 he was selected to read at the Poetry Ireland Introductions series.

His blog can be read at www.michaeljwhelan.wordpress.com.